REAL MADRID
THE MOST SUCCESSFUL CLUB
IN THE WORLD

Abbeville Press Publishers
New York · London

A portion of the book's proceeds are donated to the **Hugo Bustamante AYSO Playership Fund,** a national scholarship program to help ensure that no child misses the chance to play AYSO Soccer. Donations to the fund cover the cost of registration and a uniform for a child in need.

Text by Illugi Jökulsson

For the original edition
Design and layout: Ólafur Gunnar Guðlaugsson

For the English-language edition
Editor: Joan Strasbaugh
Production manager: Louise Kurtz
Designer: Ada Rodriguez
Copy editor: Ken Samuelson

PHOTOGRAPHY CREDITS

Getty Images
1 Champions: Shaun Botterill. 16, 17 1960 European Champions: Keystone – France.
23 1966 European Champions: Rolls Press/Popperfoto. 26, 27 The team on May 29, 1985: Bob Thomas. 28, 29 Zamorano: Lutz Bongarts. 31 Raúl: Popperfoto. 32, 33 Galacticos: Christof Koepsel. 34, 35 Zidane: Martin Rose. 42, 43 The competitors: Victor Carretero.

Shutterstock
8, 9, 10, 11, 24, 25, 36, 37, 38, 39, 40, 41, 44, 45, 46, 47, 48, 49, 50, 51, 52, 53, 54, 55.

Real Madrid Museum
6, 12 and 13. Small image.

Please note: This book has not been authorized by **Real Madrid** nor persons associated with the team, apart from images obtained from the Real Madrid Museum.

All statistics current through the 2012–2013 season unless otherwise noted.

First published in the United States of America in 2014 by Abbeville Press, 137 Varick Street, New York, NY 10013

First published in Iceland in 2012 by Sögur útgáfa, Fákafen 9, 108 Reykjavík, Iceland

First edition
10 9 8 7 6 5 4 3 2 1

Library of Congress Cataloging-in-Publication Data

Illugi Jvkulsson.
  [Real Madrid. English]
  Real Madrid :b the most successful club in the world / by Illugi Jvkulsson. — First edition.
     pages cm. — (World soccer legends)
  Translated from Icelandic.
  ISBN-13: 978-0-7892-1160-6 (hardback)
  1. Real Madrid Club de Futbol—History—Juvenile literature. I. Title.
  GV943.6.R35I5513 2014
  796.33409—dc23

                                         2013045840

For bulk and premium sales and for text adoption procedures, write to Customer Service Manager, Abbeville Press, 137 Varick Street, New York, NY 10013, or call 1-800-ARTBOOK.

Visit Abbeville Press online at **www.abbeville.com**.

CONTENTS

MADRID

It's unclear what the name Madrid means. It probably has something to do with water. The city's origins can be traced back to a fortress built by the Moors by the banks of the river Manzanares 1,200 years ago. The Moors were Muslims from North Africa who invaded Spain and ruled the country for centuries. In 1085, the Christians conquered the city and the Muslims and Jews were driven away. Madrid continued to flourish, and in 1561 King Philip II of Spain moved his court to the city. Madrid has been the capital city of Spain ever since.

Spain accumulated a lot of wealth in the following centuries from its colonies in the Americas. Many magnificent palaces were built in Madrid, and it became one of Europe's leading cities. Today the colonies have long been independent of Spain, but Madrid remains one of the largest cities in Europe.

Moors from North Africa founded Madrid.

Carlos III of Spain (1759–1788) is credited with making Madrid the splendid metropolis it is today.

47 million people live in Spain.

LARGEST CITIES IN EUROPE

1.	Istanbul, Turkey	13.9
2.	Moscow, Russia	11.5
3.	London, England	8.3
4.	St. Petersburg, Russia	4.9
5.	Berlin, Germany	3.4
6.	MADRID	3.2

The numbers indicate millions of citizens. The next cities on the list are Rome, Paris, and Bucharest, Romania.

RIVALS IN MADRID

Real is not the only soccer club in Madrid. Atlético Madrid is also a massive club and the third most successful in Spain after Real and Barcelona. Atlético has won the Liga title 9 times and the Copa del Rey 10 times. Matches between Real and Atlético are always sensational. They are called *El Derbi madrileño*. In recent years, Real has been the stronger of the two, winning almost every Derbi. Atlético supporters maintain that Real is the club of the establishment and the rich, while Atlético is more representative of the working class. Though there may have

Atlético jersey

been some truth to that in the past, the distinction is questionable today.

Rayo Vallecano is another club in Madrid. It tends to move back and forth between the first and second divisions. Then there's Getafe, in the neighboring city of that name in the metropolitan area of Madrid. It's a young club that has been doing very well in La Liga lately. The little team Alcorcón is also based in the Madrid area. It is reasonably strong but has never reached the top league. It is famous for defeating the very strong Real Madrid team in the 2009 Copa del Rey.

R. Vallecano jersey

The royal palace in Madrid

ORIGINS

Modern association football, also called soccer, originated in the middle of the 19th century in England. English students and emigrants then introduced the sport wherever they went. In 1895, students and teachers at the Institución Libre de Enseñanza in Madrid founded a team they called Football Club Sky. Many of the founders were from England. The club split twice in the following 7 years, and in 1902 a new club, called Sociedad Madrid FC, was formed. Its name later evolved into Real Madrid.

The club started out quite well. La Liga had not yet been established in Spain, but there were smaller tournaments and competitions in the various regions. The Copa del Rey, the Spanish Cup, was the only one that was open to clubs from all over the country. The new club from Madrid won the cup 4 consecutive times, from 1905 to 1908. But things went downhill from there. Real didn't win anything for a long time, except their 5th cup in 1917. Clubs like Barcelona and Athletic Bilbao eclipsed Real, and even Atlético Madrid seemed stronger than Real for a while. When the Spanish league, La Liga, was founded in 1929, Real took second place after FC Barcelona. But

just 2 years later, in the 1931–1932 season, Real became Spanish champions for the first time, and finished on top again the following year. The team then added 2 Copa del Rey titles to its trophy cabinet, in 1934 and 1936. The club was finally stirring after a long slumber. Yet it took more than a decade for Real to really blossom.

A ROYAL CLUB

For its first 18 years, the club was simply called Madrid. Its name was changed to Real Madrid in 1920, when King Alfonso XIII granted the club royal patronage. *Real* simply means "royal". When Alfonso was deposed in 1931 and a republic was established, it no longer seemed appropriate for the club to use the "Real", and for the next few years it was simply called Madrid CF. (CF is an abbreviation for "Club de Fútbol.") When the dictator Francisco Franco seized power in Spain in 1939, he granted the club permission to use the "Real" again.

THE WHITES

Real's jersey has always been white, but in the early days the socks were black, not white as they are today. For some years in the early days, the white jerseys had a diagonal blue stripe across the chest. In 1925, the club played in black shorts, but after some bad defeats against Barcelona in the Copa del Rey, the black shorts were abandoned.

THE REAL CREST

The blue stripe is reminiscent of the diagonal stripe on the club's very first jersey.

NICKNAMES

The players and supporters of Real Madrid have various nicknames in Spain. The most common one is "Los Blancos," meaning "The Whites." Then there's "Los Merengues," which refers to the snow-white French dessert made from egg whites and sugar, and is of course

inspired by Real's all-white uniform. "Los Vikingos" was coined by a reporter from *The Times* of London who described the club's team as Vikings, devastating all opposition, after the club won its 5th European Cup in 1960.

ALFONSO XIII

Alfonso XIII, the king who granted the club the venerable prefix "Real," was monarch from birth, as his father had died before he was born.

Alfonso III was passionate about soccer and granted patronage to many clubs in Spain, thus adding the prefix "Real" to their names, as with Real Sociedad, Real Betis, and Real Zaragoza.

He was deposed in 1931 and died in exile in 1941. His grandson, Juan Carlos, reclaimed the throne upon the death of the dictator General Franco in 1975.

ENTER BERNABÉU

On March 3, 1912, Madrid played a friendly match against the English Sports Club. Madrid won 2–1, and the winning goal was scored by a 16-year-old who was playing his first competitive game. This teenager would win several more matches for his club. And it's safe to say that nobody else has played as pivotal a role in the 110-year history of Real.

His name was Santiago Bernabéu Yesté, and he was born in 1895. His two older brothers were on the Real team and got him to join. He turned out to be an outstanding scorer, and until 1927 he was one of the very best players in Real's ranks. He is recorded to have played 689 matches (not all official) and scored 341 goals.

By the time Bernabéu retired from playing, he had managed to complete a degree in law. However, he continued to work for the club until 1936, when professional soccer ceased to be played in Spain, on account of the Spanish Civil War.

After the war ended in 1939, the rebuilding of Real started slowly. Atlético was the stronger club in Madrid for several years. But in 1943 Real won a controversial match against Barcelona in the Copa del Rey semifinals. Real had lost the first match 3–0, and Barcelona seemed to have secured a place in the final. However, in the second match, on June 13, Real won 11–1 in Madrid!

Barcelona maintains that, at halftime in the 1943 match, their team was paid a visit from Franco's thugs, who threatened to harm the players and their families unless they lost the match. That may be true, but Real Madrid's performance was still spectacular.

Santiago Bernabéu during his days as a player

This is still the largest winning margin ever in a "Clásico," as matches between Real and Barcelona are known.

The violent aftermath among the opposing clubs' supporters ended with government intervention, and both club presidents were ordered to step down. Real's management then looked to Santiago

Real's first team

Bernabéu for help. He was asked to take over as president of Real Madrid—which he did, and changed the club's history.

Santiago Bernabéu was a man who got things done. He reorganized the whole club, and was incredibly resolute and ambitious. For instance, he had a huge stadium built for the club. He was determined to raise Real Madrid from the ashes and make it one of the strongest clubs in Europe. He recruited some of Spain's best players, and then went on to buy international talent for Real. In 1951, he had his mind set on the superb Hungarian player László Kubala, but Barcelona "stole" him before the contract was finalized. Bernabéu got his revenge a couple of years later, when he stole Alfredo di Stéfano from Barcelona, who thought they had secured a contract with the Argentine. He also acquired another fantastic Hungarian player, Ferenc Puskás. In the 1953–1954 season, Real won La Liga for the first time since 1933. Di Stéfano was the top scorer in Spain—and not for the last time.

(Barcelona's Kubala came in second.) And in the 15 years that followed, Real secured the trophy 10 times.

But while the team from Madrid dominated La Liga for years, it was Real's magnificent achievements in Europe that made it the most famous and popular club in the world. In fact, when the European Football Association started the European Cup (now the Champions League) in 1956, Real Madrid won the competition for the first 5 years running!

Bernabéu with the trophies his team won

TRIUMPHS IN EUROPE

The Second

Di Stéfano displayed his amazing strength and vision in the preliminary rounds, especially in a famous 5–3 aggregate victory against Manchester United in the semifinals. Fiorentina from Italy struggled with the Swedish club Norrköping in the first round, but then made it to the final. With 124,000 supporters cheering them on, Di Stéfano and his teammates managed to break down the powerful Fiorentina defense and hold on to Real's title.

1
EUROPEAN CUP

June 13, 1956
Parc des Princes, Paris, France

REAL MADRID – STADE DE REIMS

4–3

Di Stéfano 14	Leblond 6
Rial 30, 79	Templin 10
Marquitos 67	Hidalgo 62

EUROPEAN CHAMPIONS 1955–56
Juan Alonso
Atienza – Marquitos – Lesmes
Zárraga – Munoz
Gento – Marsal – Rial – Di Stéfano – Joseíto

The First

Real was off to a bad start in the first European Cup final. The strong French team scored 2 goals in the first 10 minutes. But the Spaniards hit back and managed to equalize the score before halftime. In the second half, the French scored again, but Marquitos scored the equalizer, and then Hector Rial finished the French off with a goal in the 79th minute. (Rial was a brilliant Argentine who scored quite a few goals from 1954 to 1961.) Real had won its first European Cup, but no one could imagine how successful the club was to be in the following years.

PARC des PRINCES
13 JUIN
1956
FINALE
DE LA COUPE
DES CLUBS
Champions Européens
MADRID
REIMS
PROGRAMME
OFFICIEL
DE LA FEDERATION
FRANÇAISE DE FOOTBALL
édité par
football

2
EUROPEAN CUP

May 30, 1957
Santiago Bernabéu Stadium, Madrid, Spain

REAL MADRID – FIORENTINA

2–0

Di Stéfano 69 (penalty)
Gento 75

EUROPEAN CHAMPIONS 1956–1957
Juan Alonso
Manuel Torres – Marquitos – Munoz – Lesmes
Zárraga – Kopa – Mateos – Di Stéfano
Gento – Rial

3
EUROPEAN CUP

May 28, 1958
Heysel Stadium, Brussels, Belgium

REAL MADRID – AC MILAN

3–2

Di Stéfano 74   Schiaffino 59
Rial 79   Grillo 77
Gento 107

EUROPEAN CHAMPIONS 1957–1958
Juan Alonso
Atienza – Santamaría – Santisteban – Lesmes
Zárraga – Kopa – Joseíto – Di Stéfano
Gento – Rial

The Third

Real was now up against one of the powerhouses of European soccer; AC Milan was in top form in the 1950s, with the Swedish trio Gunnar Gren, Gunnar Nordahl, and Nils Liedholm on board. Liedholm was still on the team in 1958 and was Milan's captain. The match was a display of superb and entertaining soccer. Milan took the lead twice in the match, but the Spaniards—driven by Di Stéfano's passion—never gave up and equaled the score. Liedholm was just as driven, and had almost secured victory for Milan when he hit the crossbar in the dying minutes of the match. Real Madrid won in extra time, on a goal from Gento. As the story goes, Di Stéfano went to Liedholm after the match, asked to swap shirts with him, and admitted to the Swede that Milan could well have won the match. Liedholm replied, "Keep your shirt. . . . The only thing people will remember about this match later on is that Real Madrid won."

The Fourth

Real struggled in the semifinals against its neighbor Atlético Madrid. In the end, Real's newly acquired forward, Puskás, landed the club a place in the final, but could not play in it himself, because of an injury he sustained in the semifinals. In the final against Reims, Real took the lead immediately, and the team's defenders managed to control Just Fontaine, the the French club's famous scorer. In the first minutes of the second half of the match, Di Stéfano scored in his 4th consecutive Cup final and Real lifted the trophy once again.

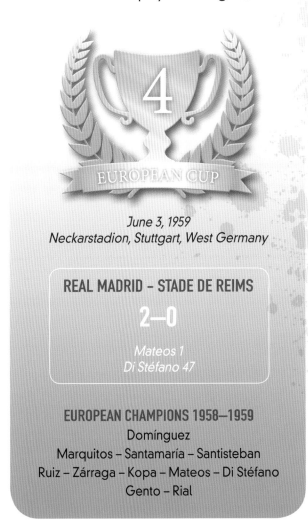

4
EUROPEAN CUP

June 3, 1959
Neckarstadion, Stuttgart, West Germany

REAL MADRID – STADE DE REIMS

2–0

Mateos 1
Di Stéfano 47

EUROPEAN CHAMPIONS 1958–1959
Domínguez
Marquitos – Santamaría – Santisteban
Ruiz – Zárraga – Kopa – Mateos – Di Stéfano
Gento – Rial

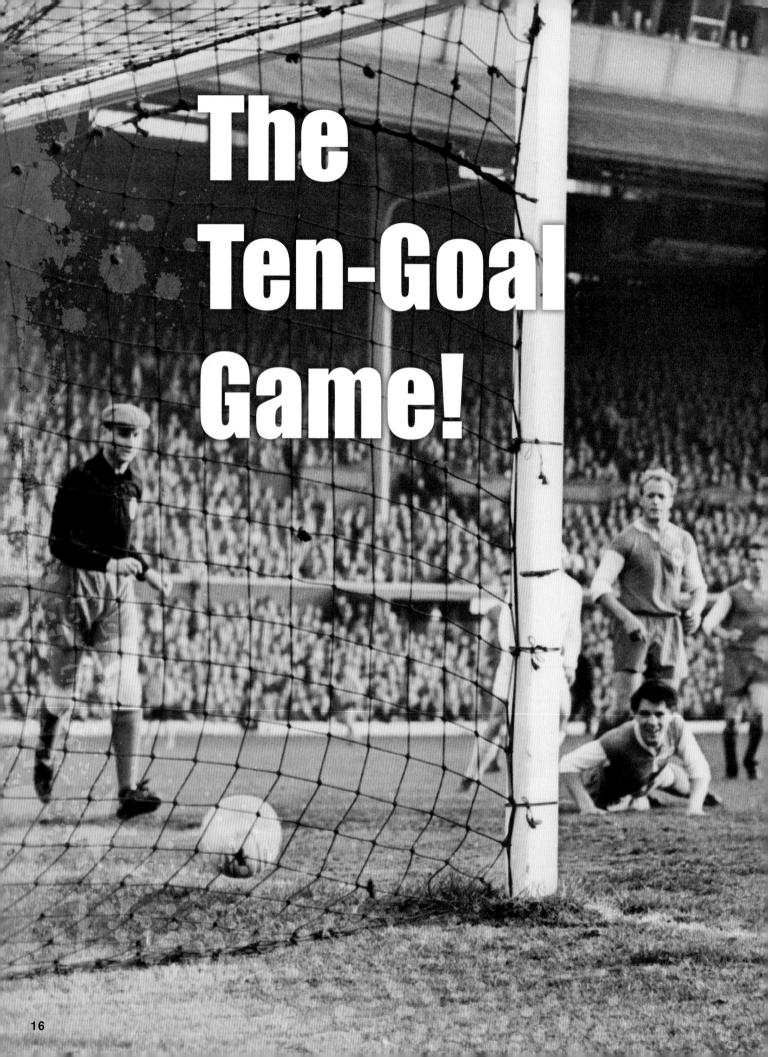

The Ten-Goal Game!

5
EUROPEAN CUP

May 18, 1960
Hampden Park, Glasgow, Scotland

REAL MADRID – EINTRACHT FRANKFURT
7–3

Di Stéfano 27, 30, 75	Kress 18
Puskás 45, 56 (pen.), 60, 71	Stein 72, 76

EUROPEAN CHAMPIONS 1959–1960
Domínguez
Marquitos – Santamaría – Pachín
Vidal – Zárraga – Luis del Sol – Di Stéfano – Canário
Gento – Puskás

The Germans had a better start, attacking vigorously and scoring a goal in the 18th minute. That seemed to wake up the genius striker Di Stefáno, who scored 2 goals in just 3 minutes. The Hungarian Puskás followed suit, scoring 4 smashing goals in a row. The Germans never gave up and managed to fight back with 2 goals toward the end of the match, but Di Stéfano completed his hat trick with an amazing run. There have never been as many goals scored in the European Cup/ UEFA Champions League final.

The German club Eintracht Frankfurt was the dark horse of the tournament, having defeated a strong Glasgow Rangers team 12–4 on aggregate in the semifinals. The Germans played vigorous soccer, and many believed they might give the 4-time defending champions a run for their money. Realhad been convincing when they beat their archrivals FC Barcelona in the semifinals, but then they lost to Barça in La Liga. Suddenly doubts were raised whether the champions were as strong as they had been. Soccer fans in Scotland were at least convinced that the final would be a match to remember, and a crowd of over 127,000 showed up at Hampden Park.

Di Stéfano scoring one of his 3 goals. The German goalkeeper, Egon Loy, does not look happy!

DI STÉFANO

Alfredo di Stéfano was born in 1926 in Argentina. He showed huge potential as a striker at an early age and scored many goals for clubs in Argentina and Colombia before moving to Spain in 1953. Barcelona had been negotiating with him, but Real Madrid's president, Santiago Bernabéu, managed to lure him to Real. The incident caused a lot of conflict between Barça and Real.

Di Stéfano scored hundreds of goals in his career for Real Madrid. He could score any type of goal, being an extremely powerful and versatile player. He also provided many assists for his teammates, such as his fellow Argentine Rial, the Frenchman Raymond Kopa, the local Gento, and last but not least the Hungarian genius Puskás, who joined Real in 1958. Di Stéfano moved a little downfield after Puskás came on board, so he didn't score as much himself but became a pivotal playmaker.

Di Stéfano left Real in 1964 to play for Espanyol in Barcelona. He continued to play well there despite being close to 40. When he hung up his cleats, he turned to coaching and won the Spanish championship with Valencia

Di Stéfano is the only player to score in 5 consecutive European Cup/UEFA Champions League finals, with a total of 7 goals in the 1956–1960 finals. This record is unlikely to be broken in the near future.

Di Stéfano
Born in 1926
Forward
Argentina and Spain
With Real 1953–64
Matches 396
Goals 307

in 1970–1971. He later became Real's coach for a time. In 2000, he was elected honorary president of Real and in 2004 the Spanish FA named Di Stéfano the country's best player of the last half-century. Around that time, the magazine *France Football* did a survey among players asking who should be named the top soccer star of the 20th century. Di Stéfano came in 4th after Pelé, Diego Maradona, and Johann Cruyff. His old teammate, Ferenc Puskás, came in 7th.

PUSKÁS

Fernec Puskás was born in Hungary in 1927. From 1949 to 1956, he was the captain and the most valuable player on his country's fantastic soccer team, which won overwhelming victories against almost every opponent. In addition to Puskás, the team boasted great attackers like Sándor Kocsis (75 goals in 68 matches) and Zoltán Czibor (17 goals in 43 matches). But nobody scored as often as Puskás himself, who netted 84 goals in 85 internationals. This squad was referred to as the "Golden Team" and is widely considered to have played the greatest soccer of any national team in history. Unfortunately, Hungary lost the 1954 World Cup final very unexpectedly to West Germany.

In 1956, the still-fabulous team disintegrated, since most of the players didn't want to play for their country any longer. The government was oppressive, and the people suffered. An uprising was brutally suppressed with Russian tanks, and thousands died. Puskás left the country, along with several other players. Kocsis and Czibor ended up playing for Barcelona. For a while it seemed Puskás's career was over, as he was over 30 and overweight.

Various European clubs turned him down, but Real decided to bet on him, and in 1958 he wore the white jersey for the first time.

Those who had feared that Puskás was too old and fat were in for a surprise. This was the beginning of one of the most successful careers of a player over the age of 30. During his first season with Madrid, Puskás scored 4 hat tricks and a total of 23 goals in 29 games. He was even more impressive the following season, scoring 47 goals in 36 games. And so it continued. Puskás played for Real for 8 years, until he was 39 years old. He was one of Real's greatest scorers until the very end of his career.

When he finally hung up his cleats, he turned to coaching but was not as successful at that as he had been as a player. After Hungary's Communist regime fell in 1989, Puskás returned to his homeland. He had always been held in high esteem, and now he was venerated as a hero by his compatriots. He died in 2006 and was missed both in his native Hungary and by the supporters of Real Madrid, who remembered all the joyous times he had raked in goals for the club.

Puskás is the only man to score a hat trick in 2 European Cup/UEFA Champions League finals. He scored 4 goals when Real beat Eintracht Frankfurt 7–3 in 1960, and all 3 goals when Real lost 5–3 to Benfica in 1962.

THE PICHICHI

The trophy awarded to the top scorer in La Liga is called the Pichichi. Di Stéfano was awarded the trophy 5 times, in 1954, 1956, 1957, 1958 (when he shared the honor with 2 others), and 1959. Then it was Puskás's turn, and he was awarded the trophy 4 times, in 1960, 1961, 1963, and 1964, when he was 37 years old!

Puskás
Striker
1926–2007
Hungary and Spain
With Real 1958–66
Matches 262
Goals 242

YÉ-YÉ GENERATION

Real Madrid's 5-year domination of the European Cup came to an end in November 1960, when the club went up against its archrival Barcelona in the first round of the tournament. The teams tied 2–2 in the first leg at Madrid, but Barcelona beat Real 2–1 in a historic match at Barcelona. Three Real goals were canceled in the match! Barcelona made it to the final but then lost unexpectedly to a new force in European soccer, Benfica from Portugal.

Benfica bared its teeth again in the following year's final on May 2, 1962. Real Madrid seemed to be back on track and made it to this game, in the Olympic Stadium in Amsterdam. Real had the upper hand in the first half of the match: Di Stéfano ruled the midfield, and Puskás scored a hat trick. But in the second half the Portuguese managed to control Di Stéfano and Puskás, and their own maestro, young Eusébio, was taking no prisoners. The match ended with a 5–3 Benfica victory, and it was clear that Real was no longer the same invincible powerhouse in the European Cup as it had been.

Real made it all the way to the European Cup final again in 1963–1964 but lost to Inter Milan 3–1. The following year Real lost in the quarterfinals, again to Benfica. In 1966, the club finally managed its 6th European Cup, but by then a new generation had taken over, and Di Stéfano and Puskás were gone.

Though Real was having trouble winning the European Cup, the club still dominated La Liga. In 20 years, from 1960 to 1980, Real won La Liga a total of 14 times. Atlético Madrid claimed 4 titles, and Valencia and Barcelona just one each. During most of this period, Real's coach was Miguel Muñoz, who retired in 1974, claiming that he'd "suffered for too long." And there certainly was a lot of pressure involved in managing Real Madrid.

By now, Santiago Bernabéu had certainly realized his dream, and when he passed away in 1978 after 35 years as president of Real, his legacy was the most successful soccer team in the world!

Miguel Muñoz, Real's coach from 1959 to 1974

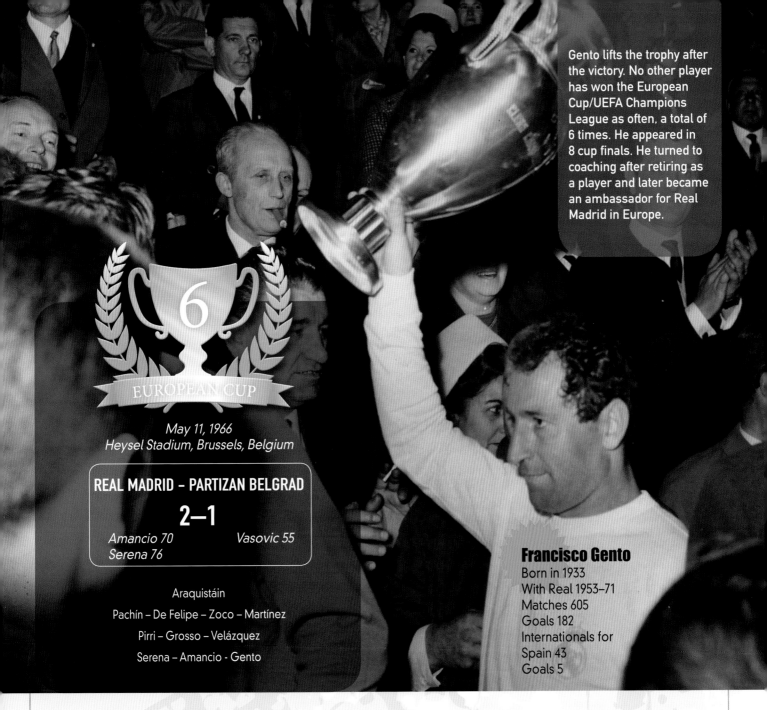

Gento lifts the trophy after the victory. No other player has won the European Cup/UEFA Champions League as often, a total of 6 times. He appeared in 8 cup finals. He turned to coaching after retiring as a player and later became an ambassador for Real Madrid in Europe.

6
EUROPEAN CUP

May 11, 1966
Heysel Stadium, Brussels, Belgium

REAL MADRID – PARTIZAN BELGRAD

2–1

Amancio 70   Vasovic 55
Serena 76

Araquistáin

Pachín – De Felipe – Zoco – Martínez

Pirri – Grosso – Velázquez

Serena – Amancio - Gento

Francisco Gento
Born in 1933
With Real 1953–71
Matches 605
Goals 182
Internationals for
Spain 43
Goals 5

The qualifiers for the 1965–1966 European Cup final were action-packed. Puskás scored 4 goals against the Dutch club Feyenoord but would only play one more match after that. With him gone, it was left to the natives to get Real to the final. Aside from the veteran captain Gento, most of the players on the team were long-haired youngsters who were often referred to as the "Yé-yé's," after the famous Beatles refrain "Yeah, yeah, yeah." They beat the defending European champions, Inter Milan, in the semifinals.

Although none of them were superstars, they certainly knew how to play soccer. They went up against the very strong Partizan Belgrad from Yugoslavia (now Serbia) in the final.

The young Spaniards struggled at first, but after conceding a goal they hit back. One of the team's best forwards, Amancio Amaro, scored the equalizer, and Fernando Serena made the winning goal for Real late in the match. Real Madrid had won its 6th European Cup, to the great joy of its supporters. But that was to be the last European Cup/UEFA Champions League the club would win for 32 years!

HOME GROUND

Real's first grounds, the Campo de O'Donnell, had a capacity of only 5,000 spectators, which would hardly be acceptable today for a large club. In 1923, the club got a new stadium called Chamartín, which seated 22,500 people.

In 1944, the club president, Santiago Bernabéu, began constructing another new stadium, called the New Chamartín. When it opened in 1947, it held 75,000 spectators. Some believed it was madness to build such a huge stadium for a club that wasn't very big or strong at the time. But when Bernabéu had made Real the most successful club in the world, there was not an empty seat to be seen in the whole stadium!

The spectator area has undergone various changes through the years. After 1954, the stadium held 125,000 people. It now has a capacity of 85,454, and is the third-largest stadium in Europe, after Camp Nou in Barcelona (98,000) and Wembley in England (90,000).

In 1955, Real Madrid's board decided to honor the club president by naming this impressive stadium for him: Estadio Santiago Bernabéu.

ESTADIO SANTIAGO BERNABEU

1902 2002

REAL MADRID C.F

25

TIME OF THE VULTURE

Emilio Butragueño
Born in 1963
With Real 1984–95
Matches 454
Goals 165
Internationals for
Spain 69
Goals 26

Real did not fare too well in the beginning of the 1980s. The club went 5 years without winning La Liga, something that hadn't happened in 30 years. The crowds at Santiago Bernabéu diminished, and even though the old legend Alfredo di Stéfano was hired as coach, things remained bleak. In the end it was Luis Molowny, a former member of the team that won the first European Cups, who got Real out of this slump. With him as coach, Real won the UEFA Cup (now called the UEFA Europa League) in 1984–1985. Real beat strong clubs like Tottenham from England and Inter from Italy on its way to the final against the Hungarian club Videoton. Real won 3–1 on aggregate.

The following season, Real defended its title by defeating the West German club FC Cologne by an aggregate 5–3.

Real was obviously back on track and now won 5 consecutive Liga titles, usually by an impressive margin!

A number of veteran players seemed to have gained a new lease on life, such as the forwards Santillana and Juanito, the midfielder Ricardo Gallego, and the great defender José Antonio Camacho.

Chendo joined Real's defense at this point and had a long and distinguished career. The Argentine Jorge Valdano—often referred to as the "Philosopher of Football"—ended his splendid career with Madrid during this period.

Real Madrid before the 2nd match against Videoton in the 1985 UEFA Cup. Back row, left to right: the German Uli Stielike, Chendo, the goalkeeper Miguel Ángel, Míchel, Isidoro, and Camacho. Front row, left to right: Butragueño, Valdano, Juanito, Manolo Sanchís, and Gallego.

Míchel
Born in 1963
With Real 1982–96
Matches 554
Goals 128
Internationals for Spain 66
Goals 21

Manolo Sanchís
Born in 1965
Matches 70
With Real 1983–2001
Matches 710
Goals 33
Internationals for Spain 48
Goals 1

Hugo Sánchez
Born in 1958
With Real 1985–92
Matches 283
Goals 207
Internationals for Mexico 58
Goals 29

Most of the credit for Real's success at that time belonged, however, to a group of young players who were all homegrown talents. They were called "La Quinta de buitre," which means "Troops of the Vulture," but also refers to the fact that there were 5 of them.

The "vulture" whose troops they were, was the brave and bold Emilio Butragueño, who bore the moniker "buitre" and was a Real Madrid icon for an entire decade.

One of the 5 left the club after a short spell, but the other 4 all played a big part in Real's dominance in Spain during this era. The player who stayed longest with the club was the defender

Sanchís, who even managed to be part of the team that claimed 2 Champions League titles before the turn of the century.

During the "time of the vulture," Real was known for its perseverance and unbeatable spirit. Some missed the spectacular soccer of Di Stéfano and Puskás, but the silverware piled up. Besides, in spite of an emphasis on sound defending, it wasn't as if Real's strikers didn't deliver: Butragueño and Míchel scored often, but the greatest scorer was Hugo Sánchez from Mexico. He had a sixth sense for finding the ball in the penalty area and delivering it into the net. Sánchez was La Liga's top scorer 5 times.

NIGHTMARES AND DREAMS

After 5 consecutive Liga titles from 1985–1986 to 1989–1990, Real slowed down for a while. Barcelona's so-called "Dream Team" became Spanish champions 4 years in a row. Real still put up a good fight, and in the 1991–1992 season the title seemed to be within its grasp. But on the last day of the league competition, Real unexpectedly lost 3–2 in an away game against the small club Tenerife in the Canaries. Thus Barcelona claimed the Liga title.

Quite bizarrely, the same thing happened a year later, in 1993. Real was in a position to secure the championship title by beating Tenerife in an away match on the last day of La Liga. And again the giants of Real Madrid lost to tiny Tenerife! This time, 2–0. And Barcelona claimed the trophy once more.

Real found some consolation in winning the Copa del Rey in 1993. Madrid defeated Real Zaragoza 2–0 in the final, but was even happier about knocking out Barcelona in the semifinals. Barcelona was immensely strong at the time and had beat Atlético Madrid by an aggregate 11–0 in the round of 16.

Mijatović

Šuker

Seedorf

Real finally claimed the Liga title in 1994–1995, and then again a couple of years later. The club was obviously still going strong. And Santiago Bernabéu was still the home ground of some superb players. There were not only the "Quinta de Buitre " but also some talents from abroad who had signed with Real in search of fame and fortune. These included the passionate scorer Iván Zamorano from Chile (173 matches, 101 goals), Davor Šuker from Croatia (106 matches, 49 goals), Predrag Mijatović from Montenegro (90 La Liga matches, 29 goals), and the Dutch midfield maestro Clarence Seedorf (157 matches, 20 goals).

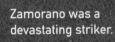

Zamorano was a devastating striker.

Two great Fernandos from Spain also donned the white jersey: Hierro and Morientes.

It was just a matter of time until Madrid's dream of a 7th European title would be realized!

"TOUCHING THE SKY"

Juanito

In April 1992, a great tragedy befell Real Madrid's supporters. The beloved forward Juanito—Juan Gómez González—died in a car accident. He had played for Real from 1977 to 1987 and was a fierce competitor who never gave up on the field. Sometimes his temper got the better of him, and he committed some rather brutal offenses in his career, but Real's fans loved him for his fiery temperament. His fighting spirit would often be the key to Real's comeback in bad situations. When he retired as a player, he turned to coaching for Mérida, and was on his way back from watching Real compete in the European Cup when he died.

Juanito played in the number 7 jersey, and to this day Real's supporters in Santiago Bernabéu will chant "¡Illa, Illa, Illa, Juanito maravilla!" (Ho, ho, ho, Marvelous Juanito!) in the 7th minute of every home game. The number 7 jersey became the club's most popular shirt.

Juanito played 284 league games for Real, scoring 85 goals. When he signed his first contract with Real Madrid in 1977, he said, "Playing for Real is like touching the sky!" These words have been remembered ever since in Madrid.

CHEESE, HOME APPLIANCES, ONLINE GAMBLING, AND AN AIRLINE

Real first donned shirts with an advertisement in 1982. It was from the Italian company Zanussi, which manufactures home appliances. From 1985 to 1989, Real's shirt sponsor was the Italian milk company Parmalat. The Whites then wore the logo of the cheese maker Reny Picot for a couple of years, and in 1991–1992 the sponsor was the Spanish company Otaysa. From 1992 to 2001, Real's shirt sponsor was the German home appliance manufacturer Teka.

Real then celebrated its 100th birthday in the season of 2001–2002 by playing without an ad on the jerseys, or simply with an ad for the club's own website. In the following years, Real's sponsors were the German electronic appliance company Siemens and then the online betting company bwin. Starting in 2013, the sponsor is the Dubai airline, Emirates.

COMEBACK IN EUROPE AFTER 32 YEARS

After more than three decades, Real finally managed to land its 7th European title in 1998, its first since the European Cup was rebranded as the UEFA Champions League. Real breezed into the final under the management of the German coach Jupp Heynckes. The opponent was the Italian giant Juventus, which was back for its 3rd consecutive final. The Italian team was considered stronger, with the French genius Zinedine Zidane orchestrating the midfield, but Real played solid defense and had some decent attempts at the goal. Once Predrag Mijatović scored an opportunistic goal in the 67th minute, Real closed ranks and won a well-deserved victory in this tough and tactical match.

UEFA CHAMPIONS LEAGUE

8

May 24, 2000
Stade de France, Paris, France

REAL MADRID – VALENCIA

3–0

Morientes 39
McManaman 67
Raúl 75

Casillas
Salgado (Hierro 85) – Karanka – Helguera – Iván Campo – R. Carlos
McManaman – Redondo
Morientes (Sávio 72) – Raúl – Anelka (Sanchis 80)

7

UEFA CHAMPIONS LEAGUE

May 20, 1998
Amsterdam Arena, Amsterdam, Netherlands

REAL MADRID – JUVENTUS

1–0

Mijatović 67

Illgner
Panucci – Hierro – Sanchis – Roberto Carlos
Karembeu – Redondo – Seedorf
Morientes (Jaime 82) – Raúl (Amavisca 90) – Mijatović (Suker 89)

After being unexpectedly eliminated in the quarterfinals of the 1998–1999 Champions League by Dynamo Kiev, the Whites were determined to do better the following season. In the quarterfinals, they knocked out the defending champions Manchester United with a famous 3–2 victory in Old Trafford, and then eliminated Bayern Munich in the semifinals (having lost to the Germans twice in the group stage). The final was against Valencia, who had eliminated Barcelona in the semifinals. That 3 Spanish clubs were in the semifinals shows just what a powerhouse Spain was becoming in European soccer. But the final wasn't very exciting; Real dominated from the start. The great scorer Morientes made the first goal with a header. The Englishman Steve McManaman played probably the best game of his Real career and delivered a spectacular second goal. Then the unstoppable Raúl tricked Valencia's goalkeeper and recorded the final goal of the match. There was some talk of coach Vincente del Bosque's boldness in trusting the 19-year-old Iker Casillas with the goalkeeping gloves for this match, but the kid didn't make one wrong move.

Raúl
Born in 1977
With Real 1994–2010
Matches 741
Goals 323
Internationals for Spain 102
Goals 44

The New Face of Real

Real experienced some ups and downs in the last decade of the 20th century. For a while, Barcelona's "Dream Team" dominated Spain, and Real struggled to get back in form. But the club worked diligently toward improvement, and in 1994–1995 a 17-year-old striker emerged who would become the new face of Real and help add substantially to the club's silverware. His name was Raúl Gonzalez Blanco, and he was born in a working class neighborhood of Madrid on June 27, 1977. Raúl wore the famous number 7 shirt for 15 years, and played more matches for Real than anyone. Raúl was the perfect forward, prowling in the opponent's box with an uncanny sixth sense for goal opportunities. This photograph of him was taken when he was celebrating the 2000 UEFA Champions League trophy he had helped win.

GALÁCTICOS

Florentino Pérez took over as club president in 2000. Real Madrid's presidents have always had a lot of authority, and with Pérez a new era began, that of the "Galácticos." These were superstars who were brought to Real on the basis of their superb performance elsewhere and their international fame. Real had always had foreign stars in its ranks, but now it became standard practice to buy some of the most famous players in the world for stupendous amounts of money. Pérez had in fact been elected president in part because of his promise to deliver the Portuguese genius Luis Figo, who was playing for Real's archrival Barcelona at the time. Pérez made good on his promise: Figo switched teams and graced the grounds in Madrid with beautiful soccer for several years, but to say that he was not welcome at Camp Nou after the move would be an understatement!

The following year, Pérez broke all records when he bought the French virtuoso Zinedine Zidane from Juventus for the amazing sum of 76 million euros. Zidane, or "Zizou" as he was called, was without

Figo
Born in 1972
With Real 2000–2005
Matches 239
Goals 57
Internationals for Portugal 127
Goals 32

Zidane
Born in 1972
With Real 2001–2006
Matches 247
Goals 48
Internationals for France 108
Goals 31

All the greatest Galácticos gathered before a European match against the German club Bayer Leverkusen in September 2004. Top row, left to right: Casillas, Helguera, Ronaldo, Pavon, Figo, Zidane, and Samuel. Bottom row, left to right: Salgado, Roberto Carlos, Raúl, Beckham.

David Beckham
Born in 1975
With Real 2003–2007
Matches 155
Goals 20
Internationals for England 115
Goals 17

a doubt the best player in the world at the time, creating openings for others and scoring spectacular goals himself.

In 2002, the Brazilian Ronaldo arrived, a lethal forward who would pile up the goals for Real. The following year saw David Beckham transfer to Madrid from Manchester United. Beckham was a superb player, known for his pinpoint-accurate crosses, assists, and free kicks, but his value lay also in his celebrity status. He was a superstar beyond the world of soccer, a household name all over the world. It

suited Pérez to have such a celebrity in the Real ranks, because it helped build the financial empire he was creating. Real was competing with United to become the richest soccer club in the world.

Roberto Carlos had joined Real before the "Galácticos" era began, but was considered one of them nonetheless. This incredible attacking left back from Brazil gave the team an interesting spin, scoring astonishing goals with his powerful long-range shots.

Real was the first club to win 9 European Cup/UEFA Champions League titles. The team easily won its two preliminary groups in the 2001–2002 Champions League, having been quite lucky with opponents. Real went on to beat Munich in the quarterfinals, and then Barcelona in the semifinals. The matches between the Spanish rivals were fierce, but Real won 2–0 in Camp Nou with goals from Zidane and McManaman, followed by a 1–1 draw at home, securing a place in the final at Hampden Park in Glasgow, against Bayer Leverkusen from Germany. Real had, of course, defeated another German team 7–3 at Hampden Park 4 decades earlier (see pp. 16–17). In the final, Real were the obvious favorites, and Raúl promptly scored the first goal. The Germans quickly recovered, though, and scored an equalizer a few minutes later. Then, in the final minute of the first half, Zidane scored the winning goal for Madrid.

And what a goal! It was a smashing volley from just inside the penalty area and into net. And taken with Zidane's "weaker" left foot!

Zizou Brings Home the 9th

This is undoubtedly one of the most beautiful Champions League goals of all time. To their credit, Leverkusen didn't give up but kept on attacking for the rest of the match. Their goalkeeper almost scored a header, but in Real's goal young Casillas was highly impressive. He came on as a substitute after César was injured, and played a pivotal role in securing this 9th European championship during the club's centennial year.

May 15, 2002
Hampden Park, Glasgow, Scotland

REAL MADRID – BAYER LEVERKUSEN

2–1

Raúl 8   Lúcio 13
Zidane 45

César (Casillas 68)

Salgado – Hierro – Helguera – Roberto Carlos

Figo (McManaman 60) – Makélélé (Flavio 73) – Zidane – Solari

Raúl – Morientes

MORE REAL FIGHTERS

The midfielder Guti was raised within Real's ranks and played a key role on the team in the first decade of the 21st century, although he was sometimes overshadowed by the "Galácticos." He was a relentless fighter on the field, a brilliant playmaker who scored many goals. In the latter part of his career, the name on the back of his jersey read "GUTI.HAZ." The initials HAZ stood for his surname Hernández, his son Aitor, and his daughter Zaira.

Florentino Pérez stepped down as president of Real Madrid for a few years, and Ramón Calderón was president from 2006 to 2009. Meanwhile, Real continued to buy strong players from other clubs. In the summer of 2006, the club acquired several new stars who would shine at Santiago Bernabéu. The Italian Fabio Cannavaro came from Juventus and was a key player in Real's defense for 3 years, the 19-year-old Gonzalo Higuaín came from River Plate in Argentina, and a lightning-fast Brazilian, Marcelo, came from Fluminense. He was a left back, brought in to replace the

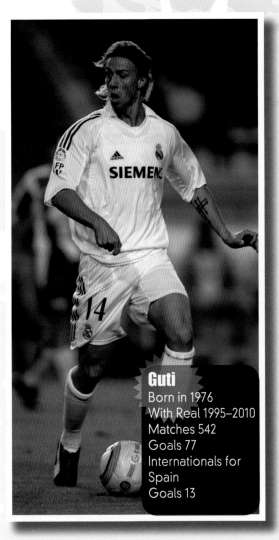

Guti
Born in 1976
With Real 1995–2010
Matches 542
Goals 77
Internationals for Spain
Goals 13

aging Roberto Carlos. Then there was Ruud van Nistelrooy from Manchester United. The Dutch goal machine joined Real at age 30 and scored a ton of goals for the club, especially in his first season, when he managed 33 goals in 47 matches.

Even though the Champions League trophy eluded Real after 2002, the club won La Liga after a bitter battle with Barcelona in 2006–2007 and again in 2007–2008, under the management of Fabio Capello and Bernd Schuster, respectively. The two rival teams were now light-years ahead of other clubs in Spain. During the first "Galáctico" years, Real's management had been accused of acquiring famous players who were not in top form, more for their commercial value than their performance. But when Barcelona started to dominate the scene with homegrown talents like Lionel Messi, Xavi, and Andrés Iniesta, Real could no longer afford to use players who were not at their best.

Marcelo
Born in 1988
Joined Real 2007
Matches 230
Goals 17
Internationals for
Brazil 26
Goals 4

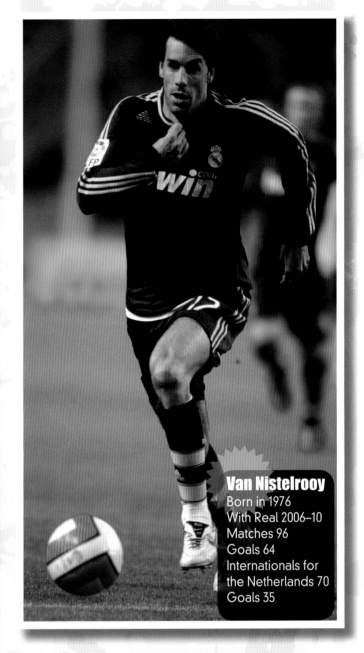

Van Nistelrooy
Born in 1976
With Real 2006–10
Matches 96
Goals 64
Internationals for
the Netherlands 70
Goals 35

Hierro
Born in 1968
With Real 1989–2003
Matches 601
Goals 126
Internationals for
Spain 89
Goals 29

While Real was often praised for playing an entertaining and beautiful game, it was also criticized for neglecting to raise homegrown talent. The forward Raúl and the goalkeeper Casillas were among the few regulars in the roster who had come up through the ranks.

There was also some regret over losing solid players like the two Fernandos, Hierro and Morientes. Hierro had been captain for years and was remarkable because he scored many goals even though he was really a defender. He left quite abruptly in 2003. Morientes was also a good scorer, but he was let go to make way for a new "Galáctico."

Morientes
Born in 1976
With Real 1997–2005
Matches 261
Goals 99
Internationals for
Spain 47
Goals 27

In 2009, Real Madrid spent 226 million euros on 4 players: Cristiano Ronaldo cost 96 million, Kaká 65 million, Xabi Alonso 35 million, and Karim Benzema 30 million.

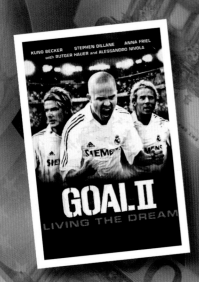

LIVING THE DREAM

The 2007 film *Goal II* captures a dream shared by millions of young people, that of signing with Real Madrid as a professional player. It tells the story of a young man from Mexico, Santiago Muñoz, who joins the ranks of the Whites. A number of actual players appear in the film, and there are even cameos from some of the great "Galácticos," like Beckham, Ronaldo, Raúl, Roberto Carlos, Zidane. The Mexican actor Kuno Becker stars as Muñoz, who gets to know both the good and the bad sides of life as a soccer superstar.

Kaká
Born in 1982
With Real 2009–2013
Matches 120
Goals 29
Internationals for
Brazil 87
Goals 29

Kaká's full name is Ricardo Izecson dos Santos Leite.

225 MILLION REAL FANS

Real Madrid has become a global financial empire. People all over the world follow the club, and according to some calculations it has as many as 225 million fans worldwide! Those who can't make it to Santiago Bernabéu to see their idols play, watch the matches on television and buy jerseys with their favorite player's name and number, in addition to other merchandise. That is a huge source of income for the club, whose net worth is 2.5 billion euros, more than any sports team in the world.

All this money means little if performance on the field isn't up to par. Real tries to ensure success by spending a lot of money on good players, and with the return of Florentio Pérez as club president in 2009, a new "Galácticos" era began. The club bought many new players in the spring of that year. The first was the Brazilian attacking midfielder Kaká, who had been absolutely brilliant with AC Milan in Italy. Kaká was bought for the second-

highest sum ever paid for a soccer player, after Zidane. But that record was broken later in 2009, when Real bought Cristiano Ronaldo from Manchester United, making him overnight the most expensive player of all time. Due to injuries and loss of form, Kaká didn't quite make it with Real, but Ronaldo certainly did!

The same year, Real also acquired Karim Benzema from the French club Lyon, and midfielder Xabi Alonso from Liverpool in England. In the following seasons, Real continued its spending spree, buying great midfield talents such as the Argentine Di María, the Germans Sami Khedira and Mesut Özil (who has since joined Arsenal), and the Croatian Luka Modri .

In the summer of 2013, Gareth Bale surpassed Cristiano Ronaldo when Real paid 100 million euros to Tottenham for his services. In spite of the growing economic chaos in Spain, Real's coffers seemed bottomless!

Real Madrid has never hesitated to spend money on talent, and has bought 4 of the 5 most expensive soccer players in history.

#	Player	Year	Transfer	Fee
1.	Bale	2013	Tottenham to Real	100 million euros
2.	C. Ronaldo	2009	M. Utd to Real	94 million euros
3.	Zidane	2001	Juventus to Real	75 million euros
4.	Ibrahimovic	2009	Inter to Barcelona	69 million euros
5.	Kaká	2009	AC Milan to Real	68 million euros

The Coaches

Real's first full-time coach was the Englishman Arthur Johnson. He played with the club from the day it was founded in 1902, and in fact scored its first goal in an official competition. (Real lost that match 3–1 to Barcelona.) In 1910, Johnson took over coaching the team and served for 10 years.

   Most of Real's coaches have not stayed long with the club. The demands are high, and if a coach doesn't deliver, he is simply let go.

   Miguel Muñoz is the exception to the rule. He started out playing midfield for the club and serving as captain. He won 3 European Cups with Real as a player. He then went on to coach the team for a few games in 1959 and finally became regular coach in 1960. Muñoz was the coach when Real won its 5th European Cup in the famous 7–3 game in Hampden Park in 1960, and he brought home another European Cup in 1966. He was the first man to win a European Cup both as a player and as a coach.

   Muñoz served as coach until January 1974. By then he had coached the team in 604 matches, which is more than twice as many as the second most successful coach, Vicente del Bosque, who oversaw 245 matches from 1999 to 2003. Del Bosque played for the club from 1970 to 1984 and now coaches the Spain national team.

   In third place is Luis Molowny. He played for Real from 1946 to 1957 and coached the team 4 times between 1974 and 1986 in a total of 180 matches.

Miguel Muñoz won 9 Liga titles, 2 Copa del Rey trophies, 1 Intercontinental Cup, and 2 European Cups.

Vicente del Bosque won 2 Liga titles, 1 Spanish Super Cup, 1 European Super Cup, 1 Intercontinental Cup, and 2 Champions League titles.

Luis Molowny won 3 Liga titles, 2 Copa del Rey trophies, 1 League Cup, and 2 UEFA cups.

The Italian Fabio Capello has managed the team twice, in 1996–1997 and again in 2006–2007, and won the Liga title both seasons. It is a testament to the tough demands of Real's management that he was still sacked, on the grounds that the team was playing boring soccer.

MOURINHO COMES AND GOES

José Mourinho from Portugal was hired as coach of Real Madrid in May 2010. His task was to pull Real out of Barcelona's shadow, as the Catalan club had dominated European soccer for the past several seasons. Mourinho had won league championships with Porto in his homeland, Chelsea in England, and Inter Milan in Italy. He had also claimed the Champions League title for both Porto and Inter. In addition to breaking the domination of Barcelona in La Liga, Real's goal was to win its 10th Champions League title. Fans assumed that the "Special One," as Mourinho was called, would be the man to bring home the coveted 10th.

Mourinho had a good start. He won the Spanish Cup in his first season, and Real was almost unbeatable in La Liga in the following season. But then the club stagnated, and in May 2013 Mourinho was fired. The Italian Carlo Ancelotti was hired to replace him. Ancelotti had won championships with AC Milan in Italy, Chelsea in England, and PSG in France. He had also won the Champions League twice with Milan.

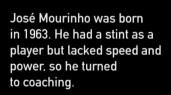

It's a little-known fact that in 2000 José Mourinho was assistant to Louis van Gaal, who was coaching Barcelona at the time. Van Gaal entrusted the team to Mourinho for the Catalonia Cup, and under the guidance of the young Portuguese coach, Barça won the title with a 3-0 victory against SE Mataró.

José Mourinho was born in 1963. He had a stint as a player but lacked speed and power, so he turned to coaching.

Is Carlo Ancelotti the man who will win the highly elusive 10th for Real Madrid?

El Clásico

Cristiano Ronaldo and Lionel Messi are the latest incarnations of the rivalry in the Clásico.

The most anticipated soccer event in Spain is without a doubt El Clásico, the meeting of the two great rival clubs, Real Madrid and Barcelona. These matches tend to be fierce and passionate. Clásico fever has spread all over the world, with hundreds of million people watching Real and Barça's brilliant players on television.

The results for the two clubs are surprisingly even, but Real has fared slightly better historically. By the summer of 2013, the total number of Clásicos in La Liga was 166. Real had won 70, lost 64, and drawn 32. The aggregate goals stood 270–259 in Real's favor. Barcelona has, however, won more Copa del Rey games. Counting those, Real has won 90 matches and lost 86.

Real once won 6 consecutive Clásicos in La Liga, from September 30, 1962, to February 29, 1965. In these victories, Real scored a total of 19 goals to Barça's 4. Puskás alone scored 7 goals, including 2 hat tricks. During this period, Real also beat Barça once in the Copa del Rey (with Puskás scoring one goal), so Real actually won 7 consecutive Clásicos in all, which is a record.

Real had experienced another streak from 1933 to 1935, winning 5 consecutive Clásicos. One was a friendly, but the others were official Liga matches. The clubs met a total of 8 times in that period without Real losing a match to Barça.

Real's biggest win was the controversial 11–1 match in the Copa del Rey in 1943 (see pages 12–13). The second-biggest was an 8–2 win in La Liga in February 1935. Real won 6–1 in 1949, and has twice won 5–0, in 1953 and 1995.

The 2 Clásicos with the most goals scored were the 11–1 match in 1943 and a 6–6 draw in the Copa in 1916. In January 1943, the clubs drew 5–5 in La Liga.

Real and Barça faced off 4 times over an 18-day period in April 2011, twice in the Champions League, once in La Liga, and once in the Copa del Rey final. Real lost the Copa final, won one of the Champions League matches, and drew the other 2 games. In the same year, the

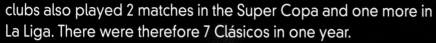

clubs also played 2 matches in the Super Copa and one more in La Liga. There were therefore 7 Clásicos in one year.

Real's top scorers in a Clásico are Sañudo (in an 8–2 match in 1935) and Barinaga (in the 11–1 match of 1943). They scored 4 goals each. (On Real Madrid's official website, Pruden, not Barinaga, is credited for the 4 goals in the latter match.)

Di Stéfano and Lionel Messi hold the joint record for most goals scored in Clásicos, 18 each. Other top-scoring Real players are Raúl with 15 goals, and Puskás and Gento with 14 each. Cristiano Ronaldo is closing in on them with 12, and he still has plenty of time to add to his score.

The supporters of the rival clubs are never happy to lose one of their own players to the other side, and they berate the "traitors" from the stands. Yet some have braved the move! A total of 17 players have transferred directly from Barcelona to Real, but only 3 from Real to Barça.

One of the most prominent recent instances was the versatile midfielder Enrique's 1996 transfer from Real to Barcelona, where he eventually became captain. And then there was the notorious transfer of Luis Figo from Barça to Real in 2000. When Figo returned to Camp Nou in the white jersey, someone threw a pig's head onto the field to shame him, but he didn't let that throw him off balance.

The classy Danish player Michael Laudrup was part of Barcelona's "Dream Team" from 1989 to 1994. He became Spanish champion 4 times in a row with the club, and was one of the best midfielders of his era. In the summer of 1994, he transferred to Real and spent 2 good seasons there, taking the Spanish championship in the first and so becoming the only player to have won La Liga 5 consecutive times with 2 clubs. Laudrup also has quite a remarkable history in the Clásicos. On January 8, 1994, he was on the Barcelona team that crushed Real 5–0 in Camp Nou. Exactly 364 days later, January 7, 1995, he was on the Real team that devastated Barcelona at Santiago Bernabéu—also 5–0!

THE GREAT GOALFEST

Gonzalo Higuaín
22 goals

Karim Benzema
21 goals

After 3 years of Barcelona's dominance in La Liga, Real finally won the league in style in 2011–2012. The club broke several records with its superb performance during the season, including the league record for points. Real lost only 2 matches of 38, drew 4, and won 32! This gave the club 100 points, one more point than the previous record set by Barcelona in 2009–2010. Real also broke its own record for goals scored in all competitions in a single season. In 1989–1990 Real scored 107 goals, but in 2011–2012 they scored a whopping total of 121 goals!

Record-breaking season!

Cristiano Ronaldo 46 goals

Casillas

Iker Casillas Fernández was born in Madrid on May 20, 1981. He is one of the few homegrown talents on Real's first team. He was just 20 years old when he became Real's starting goalkeeper, which is unusual for such a large club, but he certainly lived up to expectations. He is very solid and reliable, and can be incredibly agile when going after the ball. Casillas is captain of both Real Madrid and the Spanish national team, and has won countless awards and trophies in his career. He is the key to the almost invincible squad Spain has sent to major soccer championships in recent years. Casillas was injured for a time during the 2012–2013 season and lost his place on the squad to Diego López. When Carlo Ancelotti took over in the summer of 2013, López kept his place, so for the first time Casillas's future with his beloved boyhood club seemed uncertain.

When Casillas was a young boy, he once forgot to post his father's soccer bets for the weekend. His father turned out to have guessed all 14 results correctly, so the family lost out on about 1 million euros.

Diego López was born the same year as Casillas, and they grew up together at Real's academy. López played a handful of games for Real as Casillas's backup, but left in 2007. He made a name for himself at Villareal and then returned to Real in 2013, controversially taking over as starting keeper.

Casillas
Born in 1981
Debuted in 1999
Matches 654
Internationals for Spain 150

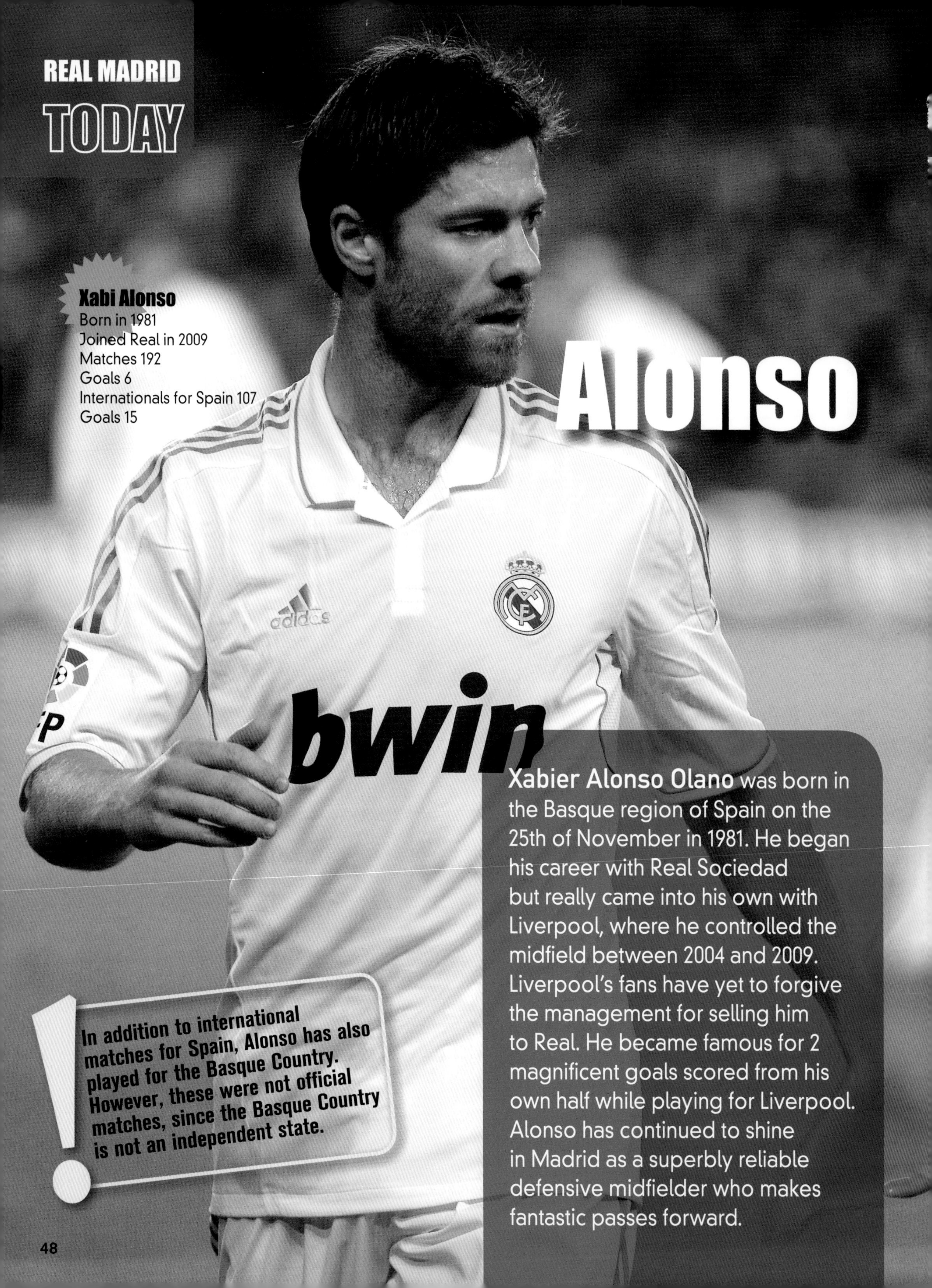

Alonso

Xabi Alonso
Born in 1981
Joined Real in 2009
Matches 192
Goals 6
Internationals for Spain 107
Goals 15

Xabier Alonso Olano was born in the Basque region of Spain on the 25th of November in 1981. He began his career with Real Sociedad but really came into his own with Liverpool, where he controlled the midfield between 2004 and 2009. Liverpool's fans have yet to forgive the management for selling him to Real. He became famous for 2 magnificent goals scored from his own half while playing for Liverpool. Alonso has continued to shine in Madrid as a superbly reliable defensive midfielder who makes fantastic passes forward.

In addition to international matches for Spain, Alonso has also played for the Basque Country. However, these were not official matches, since the Basque Country is not an independent state.

Ramos

Ramos
Born in 1986
With Real since 2005
Matches 352
Goals 41
Internationals for Spain 109
Goals 9

Sergio Ramos García was born in Seville on March 30, 1986. He began his career with Sevilla but was bought by Real for a handsome sum. He is a passionate and hardworking defender who also has an instinct for goal opportunities. He plays as a fullback or right back. He is one of the few Spanish players on the Real team in recent years, and is also part of Spain's national squad. In March 2013, he became the youngest European player to make 100 appearances with a national team.

Ramos and Jesus Navas, his teammate on the Spanish national squad, were friends and neighbors as boys.

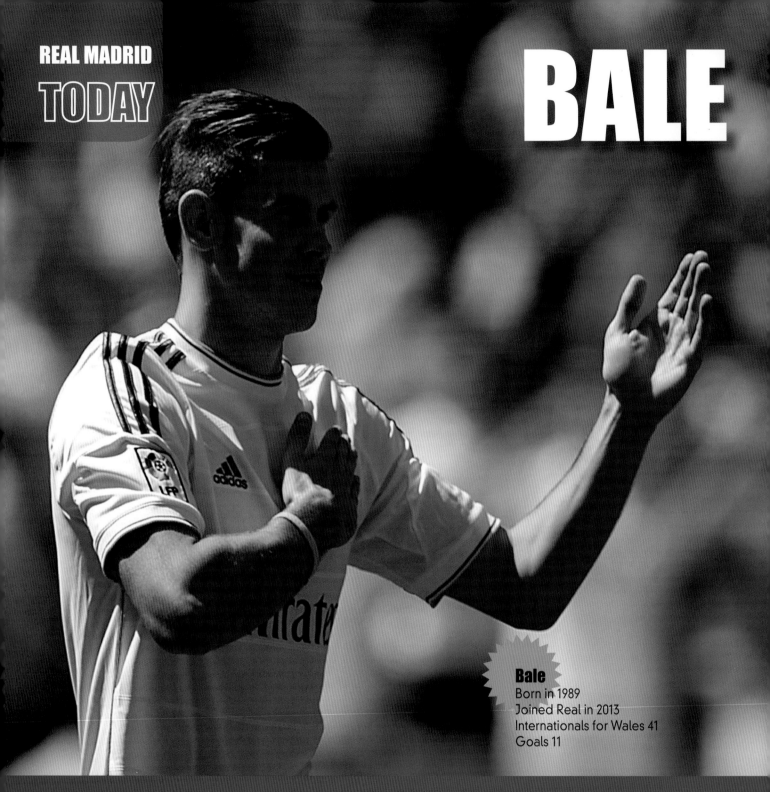

BALE

Bale
Born in 1989
Joined Real in 2013
Internationals for Wales 41
Goals 11

The powerful Welsh forward **Gareth Bale** became the world's most expensive soccer player when Real bought him from Tottenham in August 2013. The price was 100 million euros! Bale was born on July 16, 1989, in Cardiff, Wales. From very early on, it was obvious that he would become a superior athlete, and he began his career with Southampton, playing as a left back. In 2007, he left for Tottenham. Soon his explosive pace and thunderous shots moved him out of the defense and into an attacking position. His crosses and passes are great, his free kicks fabulous, and his singlemindness legendary. He should feel right at home at Santiago Bernabéu.

ISCO

The Spanish website Marca.com said: "Isco combines strength and skill. His centre of gravity is low and this makes him quick off the mark and able to keep possession of the ball, characteristics he shares with Agüero. He has great vision as well as a killer pass, and a level of control reminiscent of Zidane".

Isco
Born in 1992
Joined Real in 2013
Debuted for Spain in
February 2013

In late summer 2013, the media's attention was focused on whether Real would acquire Gareth Bale. But earlier in the summer, one of Spain's most promising and exciting players had already joined the ranks of the Madridistas. This was **Francisco Román Alarcón Suárez,** usually known as Isco. He originally came up through the ranks of Valencia but then made quite a stir as an attacking midfielder for Málaga CF. His debut for Real couldn't have been more successful, as he scored the winning goal in the 85th minute of a tough match against Real Betis in the first round of La Liga's 2013–2014 season. He then scored 2 goals against Bilbao 2 weeks later. Isco could very well become a Real legend!

DI MARÍA

Di María
Born in 1988
Joined Real in 2010
Matches 137
Goals 25
Internationals for Argentina 39
Goals 8

Ángel Fabián di María Hernández was born in Rosario, Argentina, on February 14, 1988. He made a name for himself with Benfica in Portugal but transferred to Real, where his agility, versatility, and attacking instincts on the right wing are greatly appreciated.

BENZEMA

Benzema
Born in 1987
Joined Real in 2009
Matches 183
Goals 87
Internationals for France 60
Goals 15

Karim Moustafa Benzema was born on December 19, 1987, in Lyon. He is of Algerian descent. Benzema was a great scorer with the French club Lyon but had a rather slow start with Real. During the remarkable season of 2011–2012, however, Benzema contributed 32 goals to the total of 172 that Real scored in all competitions.

TODAY

Cristiano Ronaldo dos Santos Aveiro was born on February 5, 1985, on the Portuguese island of Madeira, out in the Atlantic Ocean. Since getting a soccer ball for his 5th birthday, he has been obsessed with the sport. At the age of 18, he was bought by Manchester United, with whom he displayed incredible technique, speed, and intelligence as a player.

It was, however, in Madrid where he truly developed his full potential and became the astounding goal machine he is today. He is considered one of the best soccer players of all time. Cristiano Ronaldo is a very driven player who is always looking for a goal opportunity. He seems able to score any type of goal, and his most spectacular goals are the right-foot "tomahawk" free kicks.

Ronaldo has a flamboyant personality, and his cockiness has caused a stir at times. But his accomplishments on the field are so great that he can afford to be a bit smug once in a while! There will always be talk linking this formidable player with other big-spending clubs, but no matter what happens in the future, the Real fans will continue to revere him!

CRISTIANO RONALDO

Cristiano Ronaldo
Born in 1985
Joined Real in 2009
Matches 199
Goals 201
Internationals for Portugal 105
Goals 40

Ronaldo almost ended up with Arsenal instead of United, but Arsene Wenger, Arsenal's coach, thought he was too young and decided not to sign him.

10 Facts

Pepillo

Alfredo di Stéfano

Puskás

Real is one of 3 clubs in La Liga that have never been relegated, the other 2 being Athletic Bilbao and Barcelona.

Real's shirt and shorts have always been white, except for the season of 1925–1926. The club's management had seen the London-based Corinthians (famous for their sportsmanship and elegance) play and wanted to emulate the English uniform. Real therefore began wearing black shorts with the white jersey. But after taking a beating from Barcelona in the Copa, Real decided that the black shorts brought the club bad luck, and so they were abandoned for the traditional white.

Real's training grounds are named after Alfredo di Stéfano. The stadium there has a capacity of 12,000, and plans are in motion to double that number. The grounds were inaugurated in 2006 with a friendly match against Stade Reims, in honor of the first European Cup in 1956, when the two clubs faced each other in the final. Real dominated the match, which ended 6–1.

The record for the fastest hat trick scored in the Real jersey belongs to Pepillo. He accomplished this feat in just 8 minutes, in a Liga Match against Real Sociedad on April 10, 1960. Two months earlier, Pepillo had scored 5 goals in 39 minutes in another Liga match, against Elche, who were crushed by Real 11–2, making it Real's biggest win in La Liga.

In January 1961, Puskás scored 5 goals against Elche in La Liga, becoming the 5th Real player to score 5 goals in a league match. That would not happen again until Fernando Morientes scored 5 goals against Las Palmas in February 2002.

Raúl holds the record for most matches played in the Real jersey, a total of 741 from 1994 to 2010. In 2nd place is Manolo Sanchís, with 711 matches from 1983 to 2001. Number 3 is Santillana, with 645 matches from 1971 to 1988, followed by Hierro, Gento, Camacho, Pirri, Míchel, and Guti. Roberto Carlos is the foreign player who has appeared in the most games for Real, 512 matches from 1996 to 2007.

Raúl is also Real's top scorer of all time, with 323 goals in all competitions. Then there is Di Stéfano with 305 goals, Santilla with 289, Puskás with 242, and Hugo Sánchez with 208. At the start of the 2013–2014 season, Cristiano Ronaldo came next with 201 goals, followed by Gento (179), Pirri (171), Butragueño (171), and Amancio (155). Ronaldo will certainly climb higher on this list. During the 2011–2012 season, Ronaldo set 2 Real records by scoring 60 goals in all competitions and 46 in La Liga. He also set a new record by scoring 7 hat tricks in a season.

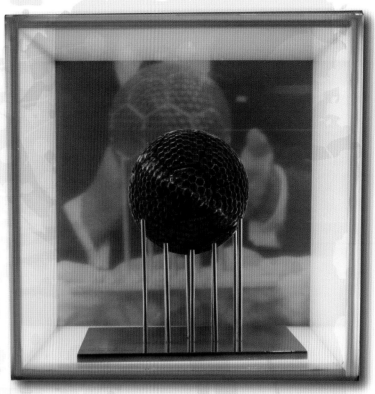
The trophy

In December 2000, FIFA presented the Club of the Century trophy to Real Madrid. Subscribers to FIFA's official magazine were asked to vote for the winner, and Real came in first by a huge margin, with 42.4% of the votes. Manchester United came 2nd with 9.7%, Bayern Munich 3rd with 9.2%, and Barcelona 4th with 5.6%.

In 1980, Real won its 14th Copa del Rey. The unusual thing was that the opposing team was Madrid's reserve team, Real Madrid Castilla. The reserve team had defeated 4 Liga clubs on its way to the final: Hércules, Bilbao, Real Sociedad, and Sporting Gijón. It came as no surprise that Real's first team dominated the match and won 6–1. Juanito scored 2 goals. After this incident, the major clubs' reserve teams were banned from playing in the same division as the first team in the Copa del Rey.

Alberto Rivera

The youngest player
to play and score for Real is Alberto Rivera, who had just turned 17 at the time. He was born in 1978 and played in 3 matches during the 1994–1995 season. He did not fare as well with Real as expected, but he went on to play quite successfully with clubs like Marseilles, Real Betis, and Sporting Gijón.

REAL STATISTICS
For La Liga, the Copa del Rey, and the European Cup/UEFA Champions League

	Winner	La Liga	Copa del Rey*	Europe
1929	Barcelona	2nd place		
1929–30	Bilbao	5th place		
1930–31	Bilbao	6th place		
1931–32	Real Madrid	Champions 1		
1932–33	Real Madrid	Champions 2		
1933–34	Bilbao	2nd place	Trophy 6	
1934–35	Real Betis	2nd place		
1935–36	Bilbao	2nd place	Trophy 7	
1939–40	Atlético Madrid	4th place		
1940–41	Atlético Madrid	6th place		
1941–42	Valencia	2nd place		
1942–43	Bilbao	10th place		
1943–44	Valencia	7th place		
1944–45	Barcelona	2nd place		
1945–46	Sevilla	4th place	Trophy 8	
1946–47	Valencia	7th place	Trophy 9	
1947–48	Barcelona	11th place		
1948–49	Barcelona	3rd place		
1949–50	Atlético Madrid	4th place		
1950–51	Atlético Madrid	9th place		
1951–52	Barcelona	3rd place		
1952–53	Barcelona	3rd place		
1953–54	Real Madrid	Champions 3		
1954–55	Real Madrid	Champions 4		
1955–56	Bilbao	3rd place		1
1956–57	Real Madrid	Champions 5		2
1957–58	Real Madrid	Champions 6		3
1958–59	Barcelona	2nd place		4
1959–60	Barcelona	2nd place		5
1960–61	Real Madrid	Champions 7		
1961–62	Real Madrid	Champions 8	Trophy 10	
1962–63	Real Madrid	Champions 9		
1963–64	Real Madrid	Champions 10		
1964–65	Real Madrid	Champions 11		
1965–66	Atlético Madrid	2nd place		6
1966–67	Real Madrid	Champions 12		
1967–68	Real Madrid	Champions 13		
1968–69	Real Madrid	Champions 14		
1969–70	Atlético Madrid	4th place	Trophy 11	
1970–71	Valencia	4th place		
1971–72	Real Madrid	Champions 15		
1972–73	Atlético Madrid	4th place		

	Winner	La Liga	Copa del Rey*	Europe
1973–74	Barcelona	8th place	Trophy 12	
1974–75	Real Madrid	Champions 16	Trophy 13	
1975–76	Real Madrid	Champions 17		
1976–77	Atlético Madrid	9th place		
1977–78	Real Madrid	Champions 18		
1978–79	Real Madrid	Champions 19		
1979–80	Real Madrid	Champions 20	Trophy 14	
1980–81	Real Sociedad	2nd place		
1981–82	Real Sociedad	3rd place	Trophy 15	
1982–83	Bilbao	2nd place		
1983–84	Bilbao	2nd place		
1984–85	Barcelona	5th place		
1985–86	Real Madrid	Champions 21		
1986–87	Real Madrid	Champions 22		
1987–88	Real Madrid	Champions 23		
1988–89	Real Madrid	Champions 24	Trophy 16	
1989–90	Real Madrid	Champions 25		
1990–91	Barcelona	3rd place		
1991–92	Barcelona	2nd place		
1992–93	Barcelona	2nd place	Trophy 17	
1993–94	Barcelona	4th place		
1994–95	Real Madrid	Champions 26		
1995–96	Atlético Madrid	6th place		
1996–97	Real Madrid	Champions 27		
1997–98	Barcelona	4th place		7
1998–99	Barcelona	2nd place		
1999–00	Deportivo Coruna	5th place		8
2000–01	Real Madrid	Champions 28		
2001–02	Valencia	3rd place		9
2002–03	Real Madrid	Champions 29		
2003–04	Valencia	4th place		
2004–05	Barcelona	2nd place		
2005–06	Barcelona	2nd place		
2006–07	Real Madrid	Champions 30		
2007–08	Real Madrid	Champions 31		
2008–09	Barcelona	2nd place		
2009–10	Barcelona	2nd place		
2010–11	Barcelona	2nd place	Trophy 18	
2011–12	Real Madrid	Champions 32		
2012–13	Barcelona	2nd place		

Most La Liga titles

1. Real Madrid 32
2. Barcelona 22
3. Atlético Madrid 9
4. Bilbao 8
6. Valencia 6

Most Spanish Cups

1. Barcelona 26
2. Bilbao 23
3. Real Madrid 18
4. Atlético Madrid 10
5. Valencia 7

* Before La Liga was established in 1929, the Spanish Cup, or the Copa del Rey as it is usually called, was the main trophy to be won in Spain. Real won the Copa 5 times before 1929, in 1905, 1906, 1907, 1908, and 1917.

Learn More!

Books
- Burns, Jimmy. *The Real Deal: A History of Real Madrid* (e-book). Endeavour Press, 2012.
- Fitzpatrick, Richard. *El Clasico: Barcelona v Real Madrid, Football's Greatest Rivalry.* London: Bloomsbury, 2012.

Websites
- Real Madrid maintains an official website, realmadrid.com, where you can find everything you would want to know about the club and its players, games, and results.
- The Wikipedia entry on Real Madrid also offers an abundance of information about the club.
- espnfc.com *(Soccernet)*
- goal.com
- 101greatgoals.com

Glossary

Striker: A forward player positioned closest to the opposing goal who has the primary role of receiving the ball from teammates and delivering it to the goal.

Winger: The player who keeps to the margins of the field and receives the ball from midfielders or defenders and then sends it forward to the awaiting strikers.

Offensive midfielder: This player is positioned behind the team's forwards and gets the ball through the opposing defense. They either pass to the strikers or attempt a goal themselves. This position is sometimes called "number 10" in reference to the Brazilian genius Pelé, who more or less created this role and wore shirt number 10.

Defensive midfielder: Usually plays in front of the team's defense. The player's central role is to break the offense of the opposing team and deliver the ball to their team's forwards. The contribution of these players is not always obvious, but they nevertheless play an important part in the game.

Central midfielder: The role of the central midfielder is divided between offense and defense. The player mainly seeks to secure the center of the field for their team. Box-to-box midfielders are versatile players who possess such strength and foresight that they constantly spring between the penalty areas.

Fullbacks (either left back or right back): Players who defend the sides of the field, near their own goal, but also dash up the field overlapping with wingers in order to lob the ball into the opponent's goal. The fullbacks are sometimes titled wingbacks if they are expected to play a bigger role in the offense.

Center backs: These players are the primary defenders of their teams, and are two or three in number depending on formation. The purpose of the center backs is first and foremost to prevent the opponents from scoring and then send the ball towards the center.

Sweeper: The original purpose of the sweeper was to stay behind the defending teammates and "sweep up" the ball if they happened to lose it, but also to take the ball forward. The position of the sweeper has now been replaced by defensive midfielders.

Goalkeeper: Prevents the opponent's goals and is the only player who is allowed to use their hands!

Coach:

Arsene wenger

Pick Your Team!

Choose Real Madrid's starting eleven. You can pick anyone you like—players from the past and present, and even those who have yet to play for Real. You can even pick yourself!

Don't forget the coach!

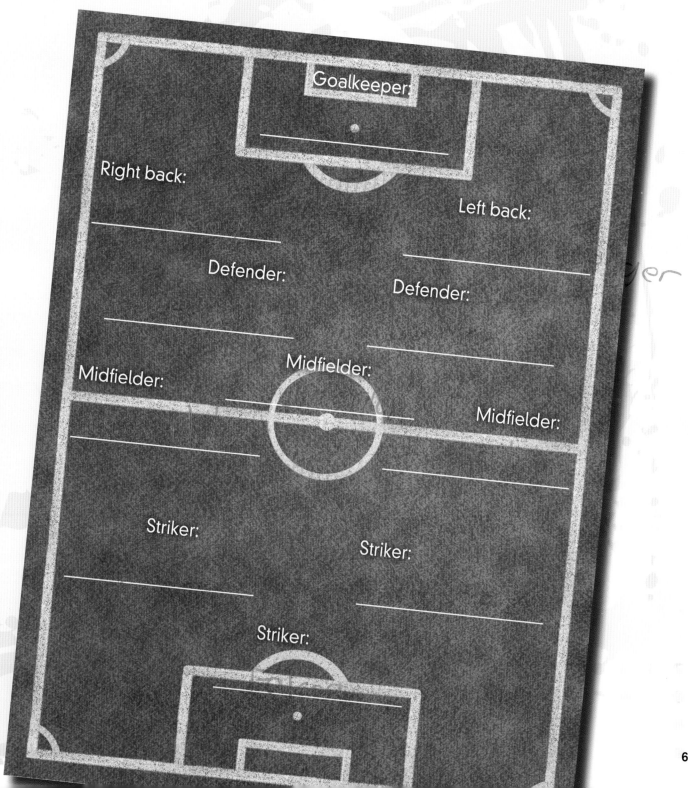

Goalkeeper:

Right back:

Left back:

Defender:

Defender:

Midfielder:

Midfielder:

Midfielder:

Striker:

Striker:

Striker:

You lose the first Clásico. Go back 4 places!

7

You win La Liga for the first time. Cheer for Madrid!

5

Play with one die.

You lose La Liga on the very last day. Wait one round.

The King grants the club patronage. Go forward 3 places.

Di Stéfano joins your ranks. Roll again.

12

You win the European Cup for the first time. Go forward one place.

You win the Copa del Rey for the first time. Go to 12!

The Real Board Game!

2

You lose yourself in the celebrations. Wait one round.

Play with one die

15

Kick off in 1902.

You beat Frankfurt 7-3. Go 3 places back and then 7 places forward.

17